Grace Lin *and* Ranida T. McKneally

Our Seasons

Illustrated by Grace Lin

◠◠◠ Charlesbridge

To Robert, who has been with me through many seasons
—G. L.

To Luke, for sharing all the seasons with me
—R. T. M.

Published by Charlesbridge
85 Main Street
Watertown, MA 02472
(617) 926-0329
www.charlesbridge.com

Library of Congress Cataloging-in-Publication Data
Lin, Grace.
  Our seasons / Grace Lin and Ranida McKneally ; illustrated by Grace Lin.
    p. cm.
  ISBN 978-1-57091-360-0 (reinforced for library use)
  ISBN 978-1-57091-361-7 (softcover)
1. Seasons—Juvenile literature. 2. Seasons in literature. I. McKneally,
Ranida. II. Title.
QB637.4.L46 2006
508.2—dc22   2005006016

Printed in China
(hc) 10 9 8 7 6 5 4 3 2
(sc) 10 9 8 7 6 5 4 3 2 1

Illustrations done in gouache on Arches hot-press watercolor paper
Display type and text type set in Ogre and Adobe Caslon
Color separations by Chroma Graphics, Singapore
Printed and bound by Jade Productions
Production supervision by Brian G. Walker

When the earth is cold
We long for the butterflies,
Yet in warmth want snow.

Why do we have seasons?

Did you know that the earth is tilted as it revolves around the sun? If you drew an imaginary line through the earth's poles, this line (the axis) would be tilted at an angle, not straight up and down. The tilt of the axis never changes, so part of the year you are facing the sun more directly and part of the year you are not. Which season you experience depends on where you live and on the time of year.

When your part of the earth is tilted toward the sun, it receives the most direct sunlight and heat. The days are long and the nights short. It is summer! When your part of the earth is tilted away from the sun, it is winter. The days are short and the nights long. There are times when the earth's axis is not pointing toward or away from the sun. This causes the less extreme seasons of spring and autumn.

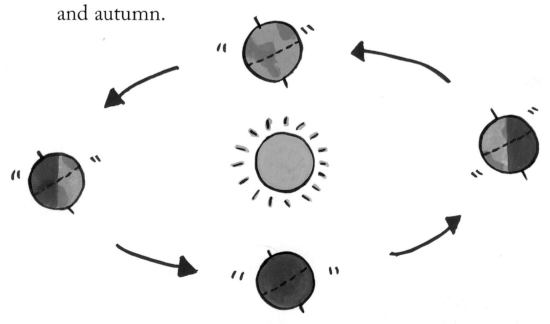

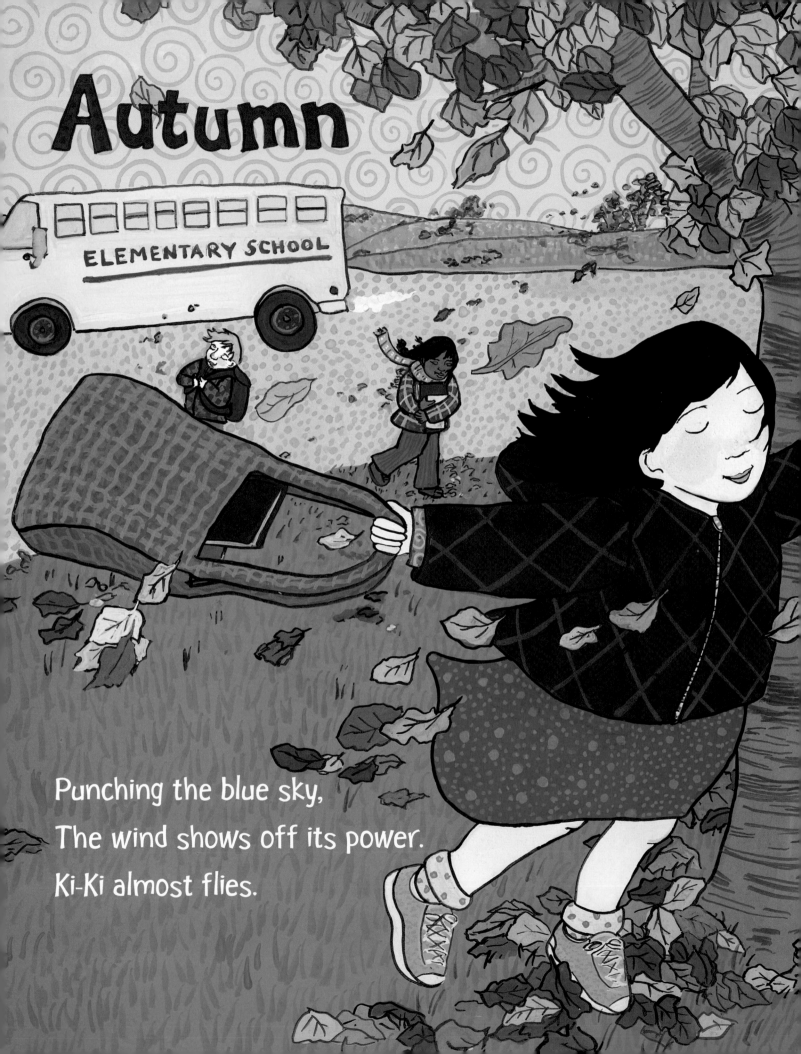

Autumn

Punching the blue sky,
The wind shows off its power.
Ki-Ki almost flies.

What makes the wind?

Air moves when there's a difference in air pressure from one area to another. Air pressure is the weight of air pushing down from above. Most differences in air pressure are caused by the sun's heat. Because the sun heats the earth unevenly, the air is warmer in some places than in others. Warm air doesn't press down as much as cold air, so we say it has low pressure. Cold air has high pressure—when air is cooled, it shrinks and sinks.

When air is heated, it expands and rises. As warm air rises, cold air flows in from surrounding areas to replace the rising air. Air always moves from areas of high pressure to areas of low pressure. When air moves you feel it as wind.

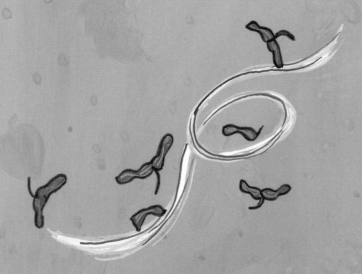

Why do leaves change color?

The color of leaves depends on what kind of pigments they have in their cells. Pigments are tiny spots of color. Leaves are green because their cells are full of a green pigment called chlorophyll. Chlorophyll helps plants use sunlight to make food.

The leaves of many plants are full of red, yellow, and orange pigments as well. During the spring and summer, when leaves are busy making food, chlorophyll hides the other colors. In the fall the leaves stop making chlorophyll and the green color goes away. What you see are the other beautiful pigments shining through.

Golden leaves flutter.
Ki-Ki tries to rake them all,
But they keep falling.

Ki-Ki sees her breath.
She pretends she's a dragon
Blowing out hot steam.

Why do I see my breath?

No matter how cold it is outside, your body is always a steady, warm temperature. When you talk you breathe out warm, moist air. Your breath mixes with the air outside your mouth.

On cold autumn days, your breath mixes with cold air. When the warm, moist air meets cold air, it condenses, turning into teeny tiny water droplets. You see these tiny water droplets as a faint white cloud.

Winter

Owen tastes the snow.

Swallowing, he licks his lips.

"Needs sugar!" he says.

What is snow?

The air around you is full of water. The water is in the form of a gas, called water vapor, so you can't see it. High in the sky, where the air is cold, the water vapor turns into tiny droplets of water that you see as clouds. Clouds are made up of millions of water droplets.

In winter, when it is very cold, the water droplets in clouds freeze into ice crystals. Over time these crystals get bigger and form beautiful snowflakes. When the crystals get too heavy to stay up in the air, they fall to the ground as snow.

Why is there frost on the window?

When water vapor touches a very cold glass surface, it turns into ice, making frost. Once the first ice crystal has formed, other crystals slowly begin to grow out from it into patterns that look like feathers, ferns, and swirls.

The patterns that frost makes depend on many things, including temperature and wind. Even tiny scratches or bits of dust on the glass can affect the frost pattern. Frost forms best when the air is very still. If the conditions are just right, the frost may look like a large, sparkly painting!

A lacy curtain
Has been drawn on the window
By the frost artist.

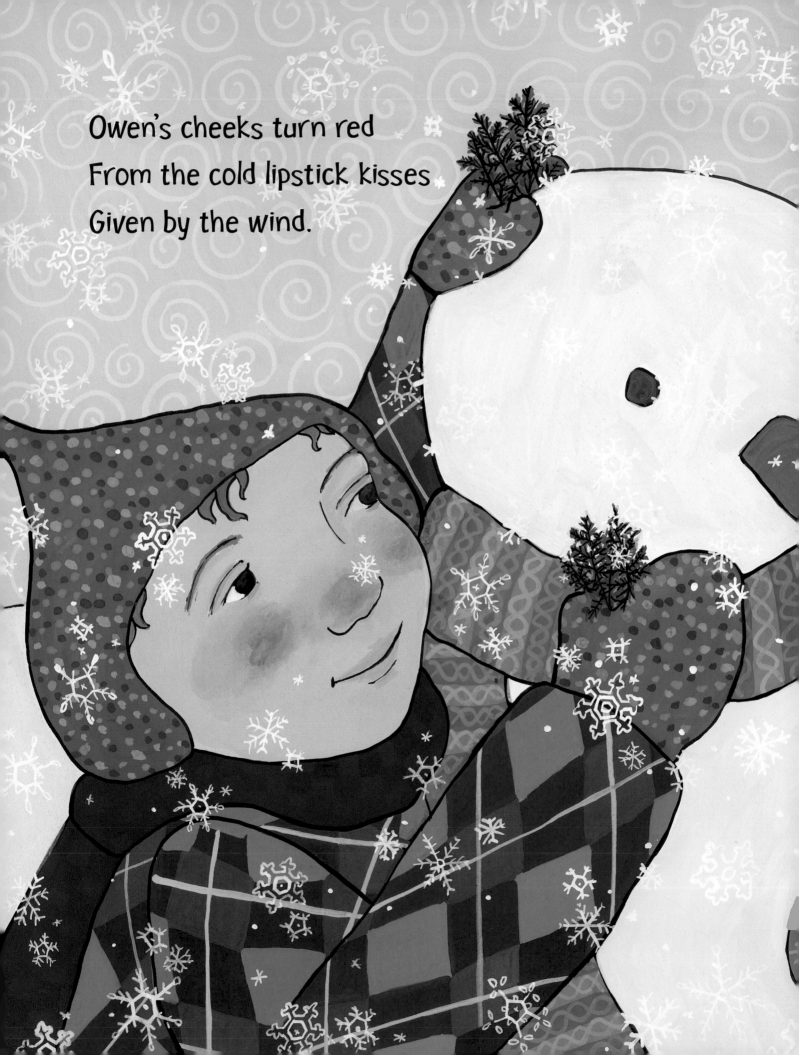

Owen's cheeks turn red
From the cold lipstick kisses
Given by the wind.

Why do my cheeks turn red in the cold?

When you have been playing out in the cold for a long time, your cheeks turn a nice rosy color. This is your body's way of protecting you from freezing.

At low temperatures the blood vessels in your face open up to let more blood flow through. Blood carries heat to your skin and helps you stay warm. When more blood flows through your cheeks, they turn red.

Spring

Lily hears thunder.

"You don't have to yell!" she calls.

Still, the sky grumbles.

What makes a thunderstorm?

When warm humid air quickly rises high into the sky, it cools and condenses into giant clouds. Electrical energy builds up inside the clouds and is released as a burst of lightning.

A streak of lightning contains an enormous amount of energy and heats the air around it to many times hotter than the sun. This intense heat causes the air to expand so quickly that you hear the expansion as a loud boom—thunder. Because light travels faster than sound, you see lightning before you hear thunder. Thunder, lightning, strong winds, heavy rain, and sometimes hail are all part of the awesome power of a thunderstorm.

Why do bees like flowers?

Bees gather the nectar and pollen that flowers make. Nectar is sweet, like sugar water. Pollen is a fine powder. The nectar is turned into honey. Some of the pollen is fed to baby bees.

New baby bees start to hatch in the spring, when there are plenty of flowers. The rest of the honey and pollen is stored away as food for the winter, when there aren't many flowers to visit.

Here in the garden
Lily looks like a flower.
The bees are confused!

The wind has fingers
That tickle Lily's pink nose.
"Ah-choo!" she sneezes.

Why do I sneeze?

A sneeze is a sudden burst of air through your nose and mouth. You sneeze when something is irritating or tickling the insides of your nose and mouth. Sneezing is the body's way of getting rid of whatever is bothering it.

In the springtime you might sneeze a lot if you are allergic to pollen. During the spring, blooming trees and other plants release large amounts of pollen into the air. If you are allergic to pollen, breathing it in causes your body to overreact. Your body produces different kinds of chemicals to help fight off the "invading" pollen. These chemicals irritate your nose and make you sneeze.

Clinging to Kevin,
Damp air refuses to move
Even with a fan.

Why is the air sticky?

Water is always evaporating from oceans, lakes, rivers, and other sources into the air. The higher the temperature, the more water that goes into the air. Therefore, when it is very hot in the summer, the air can get very moist, or humid. Air movements can bring moist or dry air across long distances.

When it is hot you usually sweat. Sweat evaporates from your skin and takes heat away from your body, making you feel cooler. When it is humid as well as hot, it takes more time for your sweat to evaporate because there is already a lot of water vapor in the air. The sweat stays on your skin. You feel not only hot, but sticky, too.

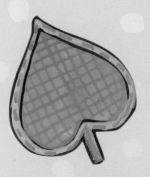

Why do fireflies glow?

Fireflies are beetles with special structures, called lanterns, in their abdomens. Chemical reactions produce light in the lanterns, making the fireflies glow.

Fireflies use their glow mainly to communicate. Different species of fireflies flash different signals, much like coded messages. They use the light to signal where they are, to discourage predators, and to warn other fireflies of danger.

In the night's darkness
Tiny lights are flickering.
What strange flies are these?

The sun cooks Kevin.

He turns brown like baked cookies.

"I'm all done!" he says.

Why do I tan?

Everyone's skin makes a pigment called melanin. The more melanin there is, the darker the color of the skin. When you are out in the sun, your skin starts to make more melanin. Melanin shields your body from the damaging rays of the sun. When your skin makes more melanin, it turns darker and you get a suntan.

When you stay out in the sun for a long time, your skin can't make enough melanin fast enough. That's when you get a sunburn.

Does everyone have four seasons?

Not every place has four seasons. In some parts of the world, there are only two seasons. For example, if you live in the tropics, the tilt of the earth's axis doesn't affect you as much. The sun hits you in about the same way every day, so the temperature stays about the same all year. But the amount of rain changes enough that there is a dry season and a wet season.

If you live near the earth's axis at the North Pole or South Pole, the temperature is always cold, but you have a light season and a dark season. This means that for the part of the year when the axis is pointing at the sun you have twenty-four hours of light a day. On the other extreme, when the axis is pointing away from the sun, you live in complete darkness for twenty-four hours a day! Many places in the world have an autumn, winter, spring, and summer. What's your favorite season?

Glossary

abdomen: the part of an insect that contains the main organs needed for digestion; located below the thorax

air pressure: the weight of air pushing down from above

chlorophyll: a green pigment in plant cells that gives plants their color; it is important in the plant's food-making process

condensation: when water vapor in the air turns into liquid water; "condense" is the opposite of "evaporate"

evaporation: when liquid water turns into water vapor

melanin: a dark pigment responsible for color in hair, skin, and eyes

nectar: a sugary liquid produced by flowers that attracts pollinators

pigment: a chemical that gives plant and animal cells (such as those in fur, hair, skin, eyes, and leaves) color

pollen: a fine powder produced by the flower of seed plants; it carries the male cells of the plant

species: a related group of organisms that share unique characteristics

water vapor: water in the form of a gas